Welcome to Rainbow Bridge Publishing's Mastering Basic Skills— "Real-Life" Math Word Problems series. Students often ask their parents and teachers, "When am I ever going to use this?" Mastering Basic Skills "Real-Life" Math Word Problems has been developed to help students see the many uses of math in the world around them. The word problems in this book help students develop problem-solving skills in real-world situations while increasing confidence in their math skills.

Content for this book is based on current NCTM (National Council of Teachers of Mathematics) standards and supports what teachers are currently using in their classrooms. Word Problems can be used both at school and at home to engage students in problem solving.

The first-grade math skills used in this book include numbers and operations, addition, subtraction, money values and time.

Rainbow Bridge Publishing
www.summerbridgeactivities.com
www.rbpbooks.com

Table of Contents

At the Jungle's Edge!

Name _____   Date _____

◇ Start Here!

Write the number word. Draw a picture of a mammal you can see at the zoo.

 1 Draw 2 _____ two

 2 Draw 5 _____

3 Draw 3 _____

4 Draw 1 _____

 5 Draw 4 _____

6 Draw 0 _____

Word Bank

zero

one

two

three

four

five

Mammal Bank

lion

hippo

camel

monkey

Name _____ Date _____

◇ **Start Here!**

Answer the questions.

 Color _____ blue.

 Color _____ red.

 Color _____ yellow.

 Color _____ orange.

Write the number.

Write the number word.

_____ three _____

1 How many are ? __3__

2 How many are ? _____

3 How many are ? _____

4 How many are ? _____

5 How many kinds of birds in all? _____

www.rbpbooks.com   reproducible   **MBS—Math Word Problems Grade 1**

Name _____   Date _____

Draw reptiles to help you write and solve the number sentence.

1

__3__ + __1__ = 4 in all

2

____ + ____ = 5 altogether

3

____ + ____ = 3 altogether

4

____ + ____ = 1 in all

5

____ + ____ = 2 in all

6

____ + ____ = 5 altogether

Reptile Bank

turtle

snake

alligator

lizard

In the Felines' Den

Name _____ Date _____

◇ Start Here!

Write the number in each box.

1

| 1 | + | 4 | = | 5 | lions |

2

| ☐ | + | ☐ | = | ☐ | lions |

3

| ☐ | + | ☐ | = | ☐ | tigers |

4

| ☐ | + | ☐ | = | ☐ | tigers |

5
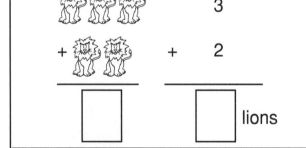

```
    3
+   2
_____
☐       lions
```

6
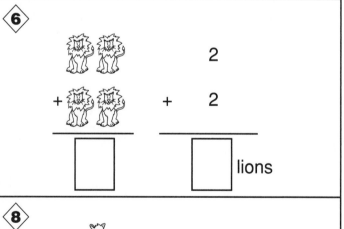

```
    2
+   2
_____
☐       lions
```

7
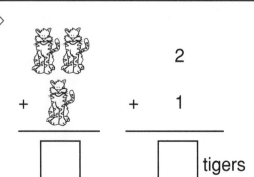

```
    2
+   1
_____
☐       tigers
```

8
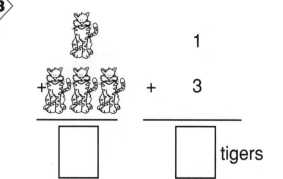

```
    1
+   3
_____
☐       tigers
```

www.rbpbooks.com   reproducible   **MBS—Math Word Problems Grade 1**

In Small Animal Land

Name _____   Date _____

◇Start Here!

Draw a picture of a small animal you can see at the zoo.

1 Draw 6 ___six___	**2** Draw 9 ___
3 Draw 8 ___	**4** Draw 5 ___
5 Draw 10 ___	**6** Draw 7 ___

Word Bank

five

six

seven

eight

nine

ten

Small Animals

bat

squirrel

mouse

ferret

Insect Life in the Tropical Gardens

Name _____   Date _____

◇ Start Here!

Write the numbers in the boxes and blanks.

1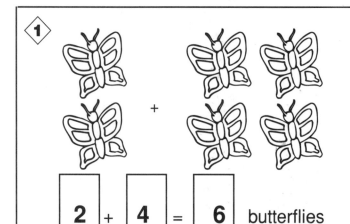

2 + 4 = 6 butterflies

2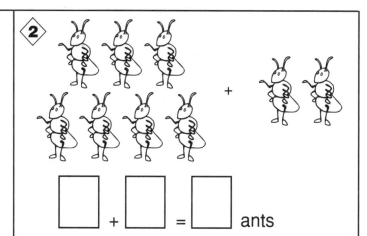

☐ + ☐ = ☐ ants

3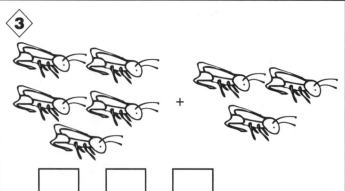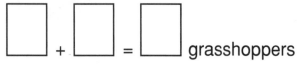

☐ + ☐ = ☐ grasshoppers

4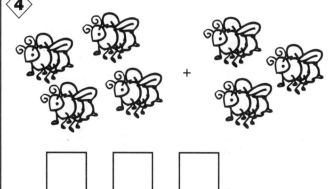

☐ + ☐ = ☐ bees

5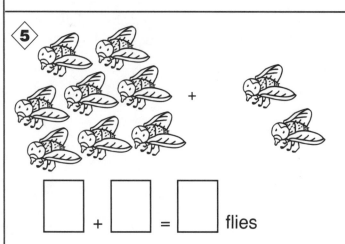

☐ + ☐ = ☐ flies

6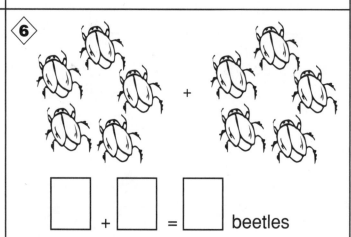

☐ + ☐ = ☐ beetles

What's Caught in the Spider's Web?

Name _____   Date _____

> **◇ Start Here!**
> Color the insects. Fill in the blanks and boxes. Write a number sentence.

1

There are 2 black flies.
There are 3 red flies.

There are ___**2**___ black flies.
There are ___**3**___ red flies.
There are ___**5**___ flies.

2 + **3** = **5**

2

There are 7 orange bees.
There are 2 purple bees.

There are _____ orange bees.
There are _____ purple bees.
There are _____ bees.

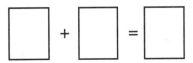

☐ + ☐ = ☐

3

There are 4 green crickets.
There are 6 yellow crickets.

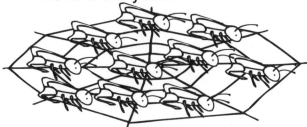

There are _____ green crickets
There are _____ yellow crickets.
There are _____ crickets.

☐ + ☐ = ☐

4

There are 5 blue butterflies.
There are 3 red butterflies.

There are _____ blue butterflies.
There are _____ red butterflies.
There are _____ butterflies.

☐ + ☐ = ☐

Name _____   Date _____

◇ Start Here!

Look at the pictures. Solve the problems.

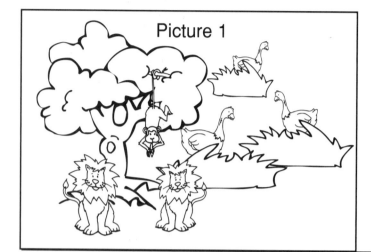

Picture 1

Picture 2

1 Write how many in each picture.   Find how many in all.

Picture 1   Picture 2

🐒 ___**1**___ + 🐒 ___**1**___ = 🐒 ___**2**___ in all

🦁 _____ + 🦁 _____ = 🦁 _____ in all

🦢 _____ + 🦢 _____ = 🦢 _____ in all

2 Look at picture 1.
Circle the set with more.

3 Look at picture 2.
Circle the set with less.

4 Look at pictures.
Circle the set with the same.

5 Write your own number sentence.

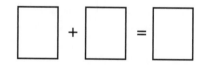

☐ + ☐ = ☐

Name _____   Date _____

◇ **Start Here!**

Count the frogs in each row. Take away the frogs that have an X.
Write how many are left.

 1

3   -   **2**   =   **1**   frog left

 2

5   -   ☐   =   ☐   frogs left

 3

5   -   ☐   =   ☐   frog left

 4

6   -   ☐   =   ☐   frogs left

Name _____

Date _____

◇ **Start Here!**

Someone left the aviary door open. Subtract to find out how many birds got away.

①   6 - 2 = **4** puffins	②  4 - 3 = ☐ owls
③ 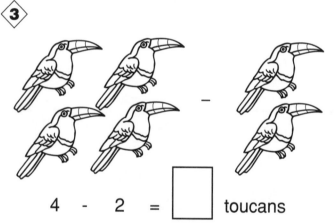 4 - 2 = ☐ toucans	④ 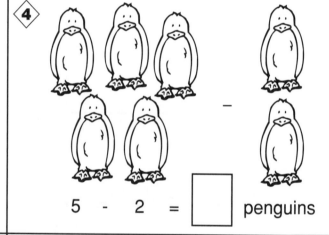 5 - 2 = ☐ penguins
⑤ 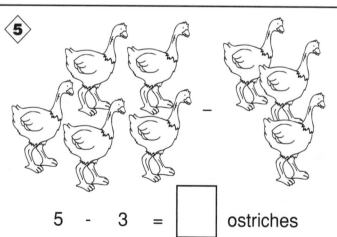 5 - 3 = ☐ ostriches	⑥  5 - 0 = ☐ ducks

www.rbpbooks.com reproducible **MBS—Math Word Problems Grade 1**

Name _____ Date _____

◇ **Start Here!**

Write in the square how many are being taken away. Subtract to find how many are left.

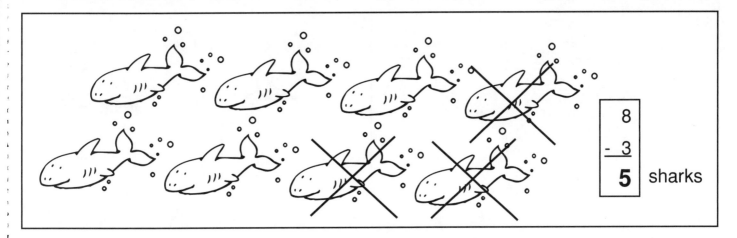

$$\begin{array}{r} 8 \\ -\ 3 \\ \hline \mathbf{5} \end{array}$$ sharks

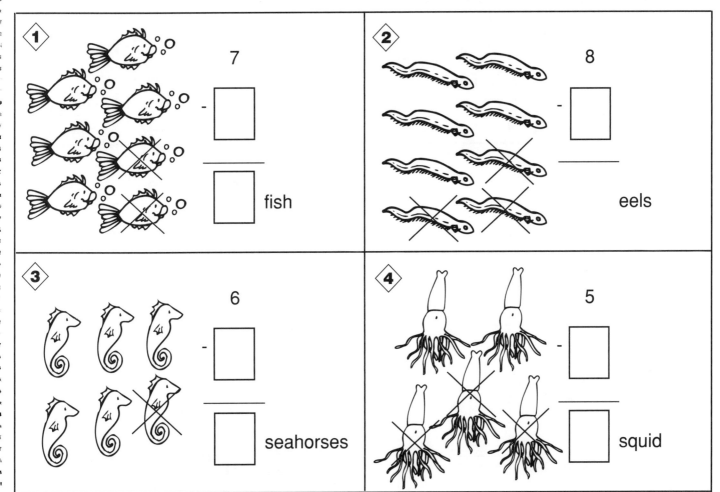

1   7

－ ☐

___

☐ fish

2   8

－ ☐

___

eels

3   6

－ ☐

___

☐ seahorses

4   5

－ ☐

___

☐ squid

The Polar Palace

Name _____   Date _____

◇ Start Here!

You choose what to subtract. Cross them out. Write what is left.

1

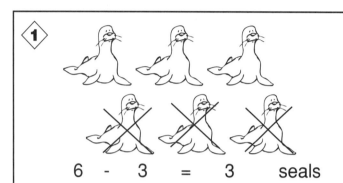

6 - 3 = 3   seals

2

3 - ☐ = ☐   walrus

3

5 - ☐ = ☐   penguins

4

9 - ☐ = ☐   arctic foxes

5

```
    4
-   ☐
_____
    ☐   polar bears
```

6

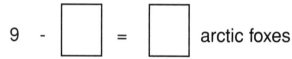

```
    2
-   ☐
_____
    ☐   whales
```

7

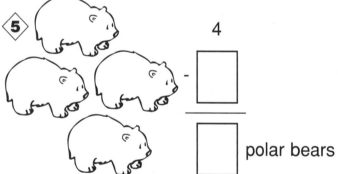

```
    3
-   ☐
_____
    ☐   musk oxen
```

8

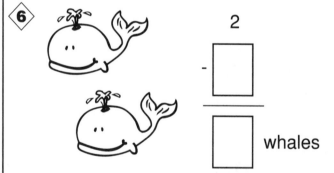

```
    5
-   ☐
_____
    ☐   owls
```

Feeding Time at the Polar Palace

Name _____ Date _____

◇ Start Here!

Read the story. Draw a picture. Add or subtract to find the answer.

---

① The zookeepers feed 3 fish to the walrus, 4 fish to the seals and 2 fish to penguins

How many fish in all?

$$\begin{array}{r} 3 \\ + \ 4 \\ + \ 2 \\ \hline 9 \end{array}$$

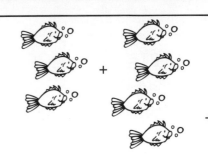

---

② There were 7 fish.

The seals ate 3.

Then they ate 2 more.

How many were left?

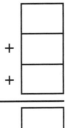

---

③ The walrus were fed 6 fish.

They ate 2 more.

Then the ate 5 more.

How many altogether?

---

④ There were 5 penguins.

Each ate a fish.

How many fish were eaten?

☐ + ☐ + ☐ + ☐ + ☐ = ☐

Picture Bank

penguin   fish   seal   walrus

Time to Take Pictures

Name _____   Date _____

◇ **Start Here!**

Draw a picture to match the problem. Then write an addition or subtraction sentence.

1 We saw 10 giraffes at the zoo. 6 giraffes were eating. How many giraffes were not eating? **10 - 6 = 4**	 
2 We saw 5 hippos. 2 were swimming. How many were not swimming? _____	
3 We saw 7 monkeys at the zoo. 4 were playing in a tree. How many were not playing? _____	
4 We saw a bear family at the zoo. There was one mother bear and two cubs. How many bears are in the family altogether? _____	

Picture Bank

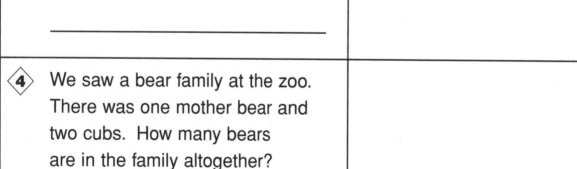

bear   monkey   hippo   giraffe

An Animal's Day

Name _____   Date _____

◇ **Start Here!**

Draw a picture to match the problem. Write a number sentence.

1 There were six lions. Three of the lions were sleeping. How many were not sleeping? 6 - 3 = 3	
2 There were eight monkeys in a tree. Four fell down. How many were left in the tree? _____	
3 There were nine kangaroos. Five of them were hopping away. How many were not hopping? _____	
4 There were two elephants drinking. One elephant walked away. How many were still drinking? _____	

Picture Bank			
 lion	 monkey	 kangaroo	 elephant

Monkeys in a Tree

Name _____   Date _____

◇ **Start Here!**

Look at the picture. Solve the problems.

Write the numbers below.

1 How many monkeys are in the tree? _____

2 How many monkeys are on the ground? _____

3 How many monkeys are upside down? _____

4 Write a number sentence about the monkeys. Find the difference.

_____ - _____ = _____ left

Name _____   Date _____

◇ Start Here!

Solve the number problem under the picture. Write + or - to show if you should add or subtract.

1

How many jellyfish in all?

5 **+** 4 = 9

2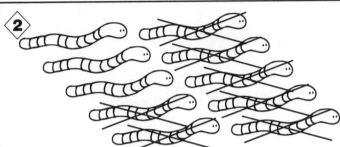

How many worms are left?

10 ☐ 7 = 3

3

How many starfish are left?

9 ☐ 3 = 6

4

How many spiders in all?

6 ☐ 2 = 8

5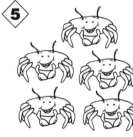

How many crabs in all?

5 ☐ 7 = 12

6

How many snails are left?

8 ☐ 3 = 5

© Rainbow Bridge Publishing   www.rbpbooks.com   reproducible   **MBS—Math Word Problems Grade 1**

More Invertebrate Animals

Name _____ Date _____

◇ Start Here!

Solve the problem under the picture. Write the numbers in the squares to find the answer.

1

How many ants in all?

$\boxed{6}$ + $\boxed{7}$ = 13

2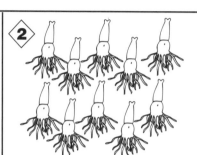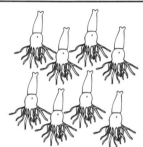

How many squids altogether?

$\boxed{}$ + $\boxed{}$ = 18

3

How many butterflies are left?

$\boxed{}$ - $\boxed{}$ = 11

4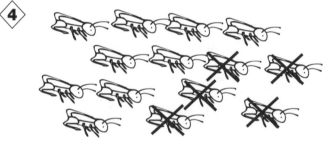

How many crickets are left?

$\boxed{}$ - $\boxed{}$ = 9

5

How many caterpillars altogether?

$\boxed{}$ + $\boxed{}$ = 15

6

How many octopuses are left?

$\boxed{}$ - $\boxed{}$ = 6

Name _____   Date _____

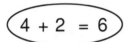 **Start Here!**

Choose the right answer.

---

1 Four seals are swimming in the water. Then two more seals jump in. How many seals are in the water now?

Circle the number sentence that tells about the story.

$\boxed{4 + 2 = 6}$ $4 - 2 = 2$

---

2 Three sharks ate two fish each. How many fish did the sharks eat?

Circle the number sentence that tells about the story.

$3 + 2 = 5$ $2 + 2 + 2 = 6$

---

3 An octopus has eight legs. How many legs can you count if you see two octopuses?

Circle the number sentence that tells about the story.

$8 + 8 = 16$ $8 - 8 = 0$

---

4 There are five seahorses. Six more seahorses swim over. How many seahorses are there in all?

Circle the number sentence that tells about the story.

$6 - 5 = 1$ $5 + 6 = 11$

Make up a story about a water animal. Draw a picture to go with it.

_____
_____
_____
_____
_____
_____
_____
_____

Feeding Time at the Reptile House

Name _____   Date _____

◇ Start Here!

Read the problem. Look at the picture to solve the problem. Color the picture.

---

1 There are 6 snakes.
2 mice are let loose in the cage.
Then 3 more are put in the cage.
Does each snake get a mouse? yes (no)

Use the < or > sign.   6 **>** 2 + 3

---

2 There are 7 turtles.
The zookeepers put 3 big fish
and 5 little fish in the tank.
Does each turtle get a fish?   yes no

Use the < or > sign.   7 ☐ 3 + 5

---

3 There are 4 lizards in a cage.
3 flies are in the cage.
Will each lizard get a fly?   yes no

Use the < or > sign.   4 ☐ 3

---

4 There are 5 crocodiles
in a swamp. 7 fish
are swimming in the water.
Does each crocodile get a fish? yes no

Use the < or > sign.   5 ☐ 7

Picture Bank

crocodile	lizard	turtle	fish	snake	mouse	fly

---

www.rbpbooks.com   22   reproducible   **MBS—Math Word Problems Grade 1**

Planning a Field Trip to the Zoo 🐟

Name _____ Date _____

◇ Start Here!

Your class is planning a field trip to the zoo on March 18. Use the calendar to answer the questions below.

March

Sunday	Monday	Tuesday	Wednesday	Thursday	Friday	Saturday
		1	2	3	4	5
6	7	8	9	10	11	12
13	14	15	16	17	18 *Field trip to the zoo!*	19
20	21	22	23	24	25	26
27	28	29	30	31		

1. What day of the week is March 18? _____

2. What day of the week is March 4? _____

3. What special event happens on March 18th? _____

4. If today is March 7, how many days must you wait before you visit the zoo?

_____

5. How many Saturdays are there before the field trip? _____

Name _____   Date _____

◇**Start Here!**
Answer the questions.

BIRD SHOW
Ticket Prices

Adult	$5.00
Child	$3.00
Senior Citizen	$1.00
Toddlers	Free

1 Draw a picture of your family. Write the cost of each person's ticket above his or her head.

2 Write each person's name, age and ticket cost here. Add to find the total cost.

NAME	AGE	COST

Total cost for your family _____

Name _____ Date _____

◇ Start Here!

Look at the pictures. Answer the questions.

Elephant Rides 75¢

Popcorn 20¢

Pet the Seal 25¢

Feed the Llama 25¢

Balloons 25¢

You have $1.00. List the things you can buy.

1	ITEM	COST

Total cost _____

Lunch at the Zoo 🌭

Name _____   Date _____

◇ **Start Here!**

Read the price chart. Solve the problems.

The Beastro Food			
Popcorn	20¢	Hot Dog	40¢
Cotton Candy	15¢	Pizza	50¢
Soda	10¢	Hamburger	60¢

1 You find some change in your pocket. Count your change.

How much money do you have? _____

2 Write what you will buy.   COST

_____ | _____
_____ | _____
_____ | _____
_____ | _____
_____ | _____
_____ | _____
_____ | _____
_____ | _____
_____ | _____

Total cost _____

3 Draw a picture to show how much money you have left.

Name _____   Date _____

◇Start Here!

Decide how much money Abbie spends to feed the animals.

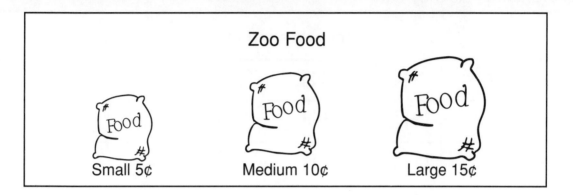

Zoo Food

Small 5¢   Medium 10¢   Large 15¢

1 Abbie buys three small sacks to feed the llama. Draw a picture of the money she will need to use.

2 Abbie buys four medium sacks to feed the kangaroos. Draw a picture of the money she will need to use.

3 Abbie buys two large sacks to feed the elephants. Draw a picture of the money she will need to use.

Money Picture Bank				
	quarter	dime	nickel	penny

Animals at the Zoo

Name _____   Date _____

◇ **Start Here!**

The class watched all the animals. They made a tally table to show the different animals they saw.

Animals seen at the zoo

mammals	卌 卌 I
birds	卌 卌 卌
reptiles	卌 IIII
amphibians	卌 卌 卌 卌
fish	卌 卌 I
insects	卌 I

Find how many animals there were of each kind. Write each number.

① mammals _____11_____   ② amphibians _____

birds _____   fish _____

reptiles _____   insects _____

③ Which animals have the most tally marks? _____

Which animals have the least tally marks? _____

Which animals have the same? _____ _____

Name _____   Date _____

 Start Here!

Answer the questions.

1 Sally checked the clock at the lion cage.

   Write the time. __**3**__ : __**00**__

2 Kevin wanted to know the time at the seal pool.

   Write the time. ____ : ____

3 Jackie arrived late at the monkey forest.

   Write the time. ____ : ____

4 Alex met John at the reptile building.

   Write the time. ____ : ____

5 Brooke looked at the clock at the elephant house.

   Write the time. ____ : ____

6 Corey arrived at the duck pond.

   Write the time. ____ : ____

Zoo Pictograph

Name _____ Date _____

◇ **Start Here!**

The class made a pictograph of their favorite animals at the zoo.

Hippos	🦛 🦛 🦛 🦛
Lions	🦁 🦁
Elephants	🐘 🐘 🐘 🐘 🐘 🐘
Monkeys	🐒 🐒 🐒 🐒 🐒 🐒 🐒 🐒

1. How many hippos are there? _____4_____

2. How many elephants are there? _____

3. How many lions are there? _____

4. How many monkeys are there? _____

Circle the answer.

5. Are there more hippos or lions?   hippos   lions

6. Are there more monkeys or elephants?   monkeys   elephants

7. Are there more hippos or monkeys?   hippos   monkeys

8. Are there more elephants or lions?   elephants   lions

9. What are there most of? _____

10. What are there least of? _____

11. How many animals did the class graph in all? _____

Answer Pages

Page 3

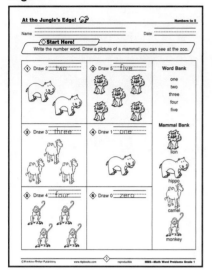

Page 4
1. 3, three
2. 4, four
3. 5, five
4. 2, two
5. 4, four

Page 5
Answers will vary.

Page 6
1. 1+4=5 lions
2. 1+2=3 lions
3. 2+2=4 tigers
4. 1+1=2 tigers
5. 5, 5 lions
6. 4, 4 lions
7. 3, 3 tigers
8. 4, 4 tigers

Page 7

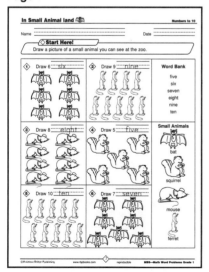

Page 8
1. 2+4=6 butterflies
2. 7+2=9 ants
3. 5+3=8 grasshoppers
4. 4+3=7 bees
5. 8+2=10 flies
6. 5+5=10 beetles

Page 9
1. 2 black flies, 3 red flies, 5 flies, 2+3=5
2. 7 orange bees, 2 purple bees, 9 bees, 7+2=9
3. 4 green crickets, 6 yellow crickets, 10 crickets, 4+6=10
4. 5 blue butterflies, 3 red butterflies, 8 butterflies, 5+3=8

Page 10
1. Picture 1: 1, 2, 3
   Picture 2: 1, 1, 2
   How many in all: 2, 3, 5
2. ostrich
3. lion
4. monkey
5. Answers will vary.

Page 11
1. 3-2=1   2. 5-1=4
3. 5-4=1   4. 6-3=3

Page 12
1. 6-2=4 puffins
2. 4-3=1 owl
3. 4-2=2 toucans
4. 5-2=3 penguins
5. 5-3=2 ostriches
6. 5-0=5 ducks

Page 13
Example: 8-3=5 sharks
1. 7-2=5 fish   2. 8-3=5 eels
3. 6-1=5 seahorses   4. 5-3=2 squid

Page 14
1–8. Answers will vary.

Page 15

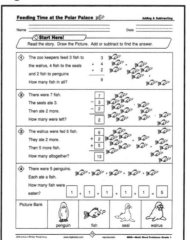

Answer Pages

Page 16

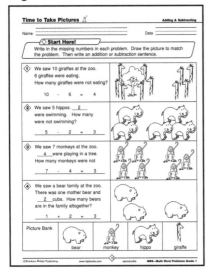

Page 17

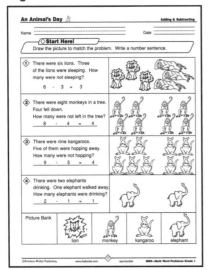

Page 18
1. 7
2. 2
3. 4
4. Answers will vary.

Page 19
1. 5+4=9
2. 10-7=3
3. 9-3=6
4. 6+2=8
5. 5+7=12
6. 8-3=5

Page 20
1. 6+7=13
2. 10+8=18
3. 16-5=11
4. 14-5=9
5. 8+7=15
6. 13-7=6

Page 21
1. 4+2=6
2. 2+2+2=6
3. 8+8=16
4. 5+6=11
Answers will vary.

Page 22
1. no, 6 > 2+3
2. yes, 7 < 3+5
3. no, 4 > 3
4. yes, 5 < 7

Page 23
1. Friday
2. Friday
3. Field trip to the zoo
4. 11
5. 2

Page 24
Answers will vary.

Page 25
Answers will vary.

Page 26
1. 85¢
2–3. Answers will vary.

Page 27
1–3. Answers will vary.

Page 28
1. 11 mammals, 15 birds, 9 reptiles
2. 20 amphibians, 11 fish, 6 insects
3. amphibians, insects, mammals and fish

Page 29
1. 3:00
2. 6:00
3. 9:00
4. 10:00
5. 11:00
6. 2:00

Page 30
1. 4
2. 6
3. 2
4. 8
5. hippos
6. monkeys
7. monkeys
8. elephants
9. monkeys
10. lions
11. 20

Rainbow Bridge Publishing
Certificate
of Completion

Awarded to

_____

for the completion of

Mastering Basic Skills

George Stark

_____   _____
Publisher's Signature   Parent's Signature

Receive RBP's FREE Parent and Teacher on-line newsletter!

Receive special offers, FREE learning exercises and great ideas to use in your classroom and at home!

To receive our on-line newsletter, please provide us with the following information:

Name:_____

Address:_____

City:_____ State: ____ Zip: _____

Email Address:_____

Store where book
was purchased: _____

Child's grade
level: _____

Book title
purchased:_____

Or visit our website:

www.sbakids.com

**Or Call:
801-268-8887**

Summer Bridge Activities™
Title	Price
Grade P-K	$12.95
Grade K-1	$12.95
Grade 1-2	$12.95
Grade 2-3	$12.95
Grade 3-4	$12.95
Grade 4-5	$12.95
Grade 5-6	$12.95

Summer Bridge Middle School™
Title	Price
Grade 6-7	$12.95
Grade 7-8	$12.95

Summer Bridge Reading Activities™
Title	Price
Grade 1-2	$6.95
Grade 2-3	$6.95
Grade 3-4	$6.95

Summer Journal™
Title	Price
Summer Journal™	$4.95

Summer Dailies™
Title	Price
Summer Dailies™	$4.95

Summer Traveler™
Title	Price
Summer Traveler™	$4.95

Math Bridge™
Title	Price
Grade 1	$9.95
Grade 2	$9.95
Grade 3	$9.95
Grade 4	$9.95
Grade 5	$9.95
Grade 6	$9.95
Grade 7	$9.95
Grade 8	$9.95

Reading Bridge™
Title	Price
Grade 1	$9.95
Grade 2	$9.95
Grade 3	$9.95
Grade 4	$9.95
Grade 5	$9.95
Grade 6	$9.95
Grade 7	$9.95
Grade 8	$9.95

Skill Builders™
Title	Price
Phonics Grade 1	$2.50
Spelling Grade 2	$2.50
Vocabulary Grade 3	$2.50
Reading Grade 1	$2.50
Reading Grade 2	$2.50
Reading Grade 3	$2.50
Math Grade 1	$2.50
Math Grade 2	$2.50
Math Grade 3	$2.50
Subtraction Grade 1	$2.50
Subtraction Grade 2	$2.50
Multiplication Grade 3	$2.50

Connection Series™
Title	Price
Reading Grade 1	$10.95
Reading Grade 2	$10.95
Reading Grade 3	$10.95
Math Grade 1	$10.95
Math Grade 2	$10.95
Math Grade 3	$10.95

Mastering Basic Skills™
Title	Price
Grammar Grade 1	$5.95
Grammar Grade 2	$5.95
Grammar Grade 3	$5.95
Word Problems Grade 1	$4.95
Word Problems Grade 2	$4.95
Word Problems Grade 3	$4.95
Word Problems Grade 4	$4.95
Listening Skills Grade 1	$4.95
Listening Skills Grade 2	$4.95
Listening Skills Grade 3	$4.95

Math Test Preparation™
Title	Price
Math Test Prep Grade 1	$10.95
Math Test Prep Grade 2	$10.95
Math Test Prep Grade 3	$10.95

First Step Spanish™
Title	Price
Colors/Shapes	$5.95
Alphabet/Numbers	$5.95

Available everywhere!
Visit your favorite bookstore.

Place
Proper
Postage
Here

Rainbow Bridge Publishing
PO Box 571470
Salt Lake City, Utah 84157

Keeping Children Busy, Happy, and Learning During the Summer and Beyond!